SIMPLE COOKERY

Quick & Easy

igloo

Published in 2011
by Igloo Books Ltd
Cottage Farm
Sywell
NN6 0BJ
www.igloo-books.com

2 4 6 8 10 9 7 5 3 1

ISBN: 978 0 85734 9 835

Project Managed by R&R Publications Marketing Pty Ltd

Food Photography: R&R Photostudio (www.rrphotostudio.com.au)
Recipe Development: R&R Test Kitchen

Printed in and manufactured in China

Contents

Lemon and Herb Scallops

Prep and cook time: 15 minutes   Serves: 6

60g / 2oz butter, melted
2 tbsp lemon juice
1 clove of garlic, crushed
1 tsp basil, finely chopped
1 tsp coriander (cilantro), finely chopped
1 tsp mint, finely chopped
500g / 18oz frozen scallops
1 red onion, cut into wedges
1 red pepper, cut into triangles
watercress and lemon wedges

Combine the butter, lemon juice, garlic and herbs and set aside.

Thread scallops, onion and pepper onto skewers and brush with the butter mixture.

Place the skewers onto a preheated grill, turning once and brushing with the butter mixture, until the scallops are just cooked (approximately 5 minutes).

Serve garnished with watercress and lemon wedges.

Greek Salad

Prep and cook time: 10 minutes   Serves: 4

1 lettuce, leaves separated and shredded

2 tomatoes, sliced

1 small cucumber, sliced

1 red pepper, cut into thin slices

1 small onion, thinly sliced

1 cup feta cheese, cut into small cubes

12 black olives

Lemon and Mint Dressing:

75ml / 2½fl. oz olive oil

2 tbsp lemon juice

2 tsp fresh mint, chopped

2 tsp fresh marjoram, chopped

salt and black pepper

Line a large serving platter or salad bowl with the lettuce. Top with the tomatoes, cucumber, pepper, onion, feta and olives.

To make the dressing, place the oil, lemon juice, mint and marjoram in a screwtop jar and season to taste. Shake well. Spoon over the salad. Serve immediately.

Carrot and Sweet Potato Soup

Prep and cook time: 50 minutes   Serves: 4

2 tbsp butter
1 large onion, chopped
3 large carrots, chopped
1 large sweet potato, chopped
4 cups chicken or vegetable stock
¾ cup sour cream
2 tbsp fresh dill, chopped

Melt the butter in a saucepan over a medium heat. Add the onion, carrots and sweet potato. Cook for 5 minutes.

Stir in the stock. Bring to the boil. Simmer for 30 minutes. Cool slightly.

Purée the soup. Return the soup to a clean saucepan. Stir in the sour cream. Cook, without boiling, stirring constantly, for 5 minutes or until the soup is hot. Stir in the dill. Serve immediately.

Tomato and Mozzarella Salad

Prep and cook time: 15 minutes

Serves: 4

6 plum tomatoes, sliced

1 cup mozzarella cheese, drained and sliced

2 spring onions (scallions), sliced

6 tbsp black olives

salt and black pepper

Dressing:

45ml /1½fl. oz extra virgin olive oil

1 clove of garlic, crushed

2 tsp balsamic vinegar

2 tbsp fresh basil, chopped

Arrange the tomatoes, mozzarella, spring onions and olives in layers on serving plates and season to taste.

To make the dressing, heat the oil and garlic in a small saucepan over a very low heat for 2 minutes, or until the garlic has softened but not browned. Remove the pan from the heat, add the vinegar and basil, stir well then pour over the salad and serve.

Caesar Salad with Prosciutto

Prep and cook time: 30 minutes   Serves: 4

4 slices, cut into cubes

4 large slices of prosciutto

2 Romaine lettuce, torn into bite-sized pieces

½ cup Parmesan cheese, grated, plus extra to serve (optional)

Dressing:

8 anchovies, drained and mashed

2 tbsp extra-virgin olive oil

3 tbsp mayonnaise

1 clove of garlic, crushed

1 tsp white-wine vinegar

½ tsp Worcestershire sauce

freshly ground black pepper

Preheat the oven to 200°C (400F). To make the croutons, place the bread cubes on a baking tray and cook for 10–12 minutes, turning occasionally, until crisp and golden.

Preheat the grill to high. Grill the prosciutto for 1 minute or until very crisp, then leave to cool for 2 minutes. Place the lettuce leaves, croutons and Parmesan in a bowl.

To make the dressing, put the anchovies, oil, mayonnaise, garlic, vinegar, Worcestershire sauce and pepper into a bowl and beat until smooth. Spoon over the lettuce and croutons, then toss until well coated. Top with the crispy prosciutto and extra Parmesan (if using) and serve.

Lamb with Mint Butter and Saffron Mash

Prep and cook time: 40 minutes

Serves: 4

910g / 2lb floury potatoes cut into chunks

salt and black pepper

2 tbsp butter, softened

2 tbsp fresh mint, chopped, plus extra leaves to garnish

½ tsp ground cumin

60ml / 2fl. oz cream

pinch of saffron

4 lamb leg steaks

Cook the potatoes in a large saucepan of lightly salted water for 15 minutes or until tender. Mash together half the butter with the mint, cumin and a little pepper, then cover and refrigerate. Put the cream and saffron in a small pan, gently heat through, then remove from the heat and let it stand for 5 minutes to infuse.

Preheat the grill to high. Season the lamb steaks and grill for 4–5 minutes each side, or until done to your liking. Cover with foil and leave to rest for 5 minutes. Drain the potatoes well and mash, then mix in the remaining butter and the saffron cream and season.

Divide the chilled mint butter between the steaks and grill for a few seconds until it melts. Serve the steaks with the saffron mash and pan juices. Garnish with the mint.

Beef Fillet with Wild Mushrooms

Prep and cook time: 45 minutes   Serves: 4

15g / ½ oz dried porcini mushrooms

75g / 2½oz butter

4 beef fillets

3 cups mixed fresh wild mushrooms, sliced

1 clove of garlic, crushed

1 tsp chopped fresh thyme, chopped

½ cup red wine

½ cup beef stock

salt and black pepper

Preheat the oven to 160°C (325F). Cover the dried mushrooms with 85ml (3fl. oz) of boiling water. Soak for 15 minutes or until softened. Strain, reserving the soaking liquid, then chop the mushrooms. Melt a little of the butter and fry the fillets for 2–3 minutes each side, until browned. Wrap loosely in foil and keep warm in the oven.

Add a little of the butter to the pan and fry the fresh mushrooms, dried mushrooms, garlic and thyme for 4 minutes, or until the fresh mushrooms have softened. Add the wine, increase the heat and boil for 1–2 minutes, until the sauce has reduced by half.

Mix the dried mushroom soaking liquid with the beef stock, then add to the pan and simmer for 3 minutes. Stir in the remaining butter and season. Serve with the steaks, garnished with the thyme.

Balsamic Duck Breasts with Potato Rösti

Prep and cook time: 35 minutes   Serves: 4

2 tbsp balsamic vinegar

1 tsp clear honey

1 clove of garlic, crushed

pinch of 5 spice powder

salt and black pepper

4 boneless duck breasts, about 170g / 6oz each

455g /1lb waxy potatoes, peeled and shredded

30g / 1oz butter

2 tbsp olive oil

4 tbsp apple and plum chutney, to serve

Combine the vinegar, honey, garlic, 5 spice powder, salt and pepper in a bowl. Cut several slashes in each duck breast with a sharp knife and rub in the mixture. Set aside.

Rinse the potatoes, squeeze dry in clean kitchen towel, then season. Heat the butter and the oil in a pan, add 4 tablespoons of the potato mixture (about half) and press down gently to make 4 rösti (potato cakes). Fry for 5–6 minutes each side, until browned and cooked through. Repeat to make 4 more.

Meanwhile, preheat the grill to high. Cook the duck close to the heat for 4-5 minutes each side. Wrap in foil and leave to rest for 5 minutes, then slice it and serve with any juices, the rösti, and spoonfuls of the chutney.

Teriyaki Chicken

Prep and cook time: 10 minutes

Serves: 2–4

455g / 1lb chicken
skinless fillets

Teriyaki Marinade:
½ cup soy sauce
2 tbsp brown sugar
½ tsp minced ginger
2 tbsp wine vinegar
1 clove of garlic, crushed
2 tbsp tomato sauce

To make the marinade, mix all the ingredients together.

Place the fillets in a non-metallic container and stir in about half a cup of teriyaki marinade. Cover and marinate for 30 minutes at room temperature or place in the refrigerator for several hours or overnight.

Heat the grill until hot. Place a sheet of foil over the grill bars. Place the chicken on the grill and cook for 2 minutes each side until cooked through and golden, brushing with marinade as they cook.

Chicken Satay Skewers

Prep and cook time: 1 hour 30 minutes   Serves: 4

500g / 18oz chicken
thigh fillets

Satay Sauce Marinade:
½ cup peanut butter
½ cup water
1 clove of garlic, crushed
1 tbsp brown sugar
A pinch chilli powder
2 tsp soy sauce
1 tbsp shredded white onion

Mix all the satay sauce ingredients together in a saucepan. Simmer and stir occasionally for 5 minutes. Allow them to cool completely.

Soak the bamboo skewers in water. Cut the thigh fillets into cubes, place in a bowl and mix in the cooled satay sauce. Cover and stand to marinate for 1 hour or longer if refrigerated.

Thread 4–5 cubes onto each skewer, spaced to be almost touching. Heat the broiler or barbecue to medium high and cover with a sheet of baking paper. Place the skewers on the paper and cook for 12–15 minutes, turning and brushing frequently with the remaining satay sauce. Increase the heat for the last 3–5 minutes to brown and cook through. Serve immediately.

Marinated Grilled Fish with Basil Tomato Topping

Prep and cook time: 2 hours 15 minutes   Serves: 3–4

4 x 200g / 7oz white fish
fillets

Marinade:

1 tbsp grated onion

2 tbsp olive oil

2 tbsp lemon juice

¼ tsp ground black pepper

½ tsp salt or pepper, to taste

3 bay leaves

Topping:

10 basil leaves

2 tomatoes, sliced

1 tbsp Parmesan cheese,
grated

Place the fish in a single layer in a non-metallic dish. Mix the marinade ingredients together and pour over the fish. Cover and marinate for 2 hours in the refrigerator.

Remove the fish from the marinade. Preheat the grill, cover with baking paper and place the fish on top. Cook for 3 minutes or according to thickness, until the fish just flakes. Place 3 basil leaves on top. Cover with 2–3 slices of tomato and top the tomato with cheese. Cover with a sheet of baking paper, close the grill and cook for 30–40 seconds. Remove immediately and serve with desired accompaniments.

14

Gratin of Scallops and Mushrooms

Prep and cook time: 20 minutes   Serves: 4

4 large fresh scallops
145ml / 5fl. oz milk
145ml / 5fl. oz cream
30g / 1oz flour
30g / 1oz butter
¼ tsp freshly shredded nutmeg
55g / 2oz Gruyère or Lancashire cheese, diced
115g / 4oz button mushroooms trimmed and halved

Trim the scallops, remove the orange coral and cut the white flesh of each scallop into 8 pieces.

Pour the milk into a non-stick saucepan. Add the scallops (except for the corals), increase the heat to boiling point and simmer for 5 minutes. Remove the scallops from the milk and set aside.

Add the cream, flour, butter, and nutmeg to the milk and beat gently over a low heat until the sauce thickens. Add the cheese and allow to melt without letting it boil.

Sauté mushrooms for 2–3 minutes.

Spoon some scallops onto the middle of each serving plate. Arrange the mushrooms around the scallops. Drizzle any juices over the mushrooms.

Top scallop pieces with corals and cover with the sauce.

Salmon with Pineapple Salsa

Prep and cook time: 20 minutes   Serves: 4

4 salmon steaks

Pineapple Salsa:

1 cup pineapple chunks, drained

2 spring onions (scallions), chopped

1 fresh red chilli, chopped

1 tbsp lemon juice

2 tbsp chopped mint leaves

Cook the salmon on a lightly oiled preheated barbecue or under a grill for 3–5 minutes each side (or until cooked).

To make the salsa, combine all the ingredients. Serve with the salmon.

Asparagus and Lemon Risotto

Prep and cook time: 40 minutes   Serves: 4–6

2 tbsp olive oil

1 onion, chopped

2 cups arborio rice

1 cup white wine

3 cups chicken or
vegetable stock

1 cup asparagus tips, cut into
bite-sized pieces

60g / 2oz butter

½ cup Parmesan cheese,
shredded

salt and black pepper

2 tbsp fresh parsley, chopped

1 lemon, grated zest

Heat the oil in a large, heavy-based saucepan or frying pan, then add the onion and fry for 3–4 minutes, until golden. Add the rice and stir for 1 minute or until coated with the oil. Stir in the wine and increase the heat to boiling point, then reduce the heat and continue stirring for 4–5 minutes, until the wine has been absorbed by the rice.

Pour about a third of the stock into the rice and simmer for 4–5 minutes, stirring constantly. Once the stock has been absorbed, add half the remaining stock and cook, stirring, until absorbed. Add the remaining stock and the asparagus and cook, stirring, for 5 minutes or until the rice and asparagus are tender but still firm to the bite.

Add the butter and half the Parmesan and season. Cook for 1 minute, or until the butter and cheese have melted into the rice, stirring constantly. Sprinkle with the remaining Parmesan and the parsley and lemon zest.

Spinach, Olive and Feta Frittata

Prep and cook time: 40 minutes   Serves: 4

10 eggs, lightly beaten
1 tbsp fresh oregano, chopped
freshly ground black pepper
75ml / 2½fl. oz olive oil
225g / 9oz potatoes, peeled and diced
1 onion, diced
1 clove of garlic, crushed
2 cups baby spinach
4 tbsp black olives, pitted and halved
½ cup feta cheese, crumbled
½ cup sun-dried tomatoes
3 large red peppers

Combine the eggs and oregano in a bowl, season with black pepper and set aside.

Heat the oil in a 23cm / 9in pan and sauté the potatoes, onion and garlic for a few minutes until soft.

Add the spinach and cook until it begins to wilt. Remove the pan from the heat, then add the olives, feta and tomatoes.

Return the pan to a very low heat, pour in the egg mixture and cook for 10–15 minutes. Run a spatula around the sides of the pan as the frittata is cooking and tilt it slightly so that the egg mixture runs down the sides a little.

Meanwhile make the red pepper salsa. Halve the peppers and remove the seeds. Chargrill thm until black under grill. Let them cool and remove the skins. Roughly chop them and transfer to a bowl.

When the frittata is almost done, place it under a grill for 5 minutes to cook and brown the top.

Serve in wedges with the roasted red pepper salsa.

Eggplant Rolls

Prep and cook time: 40 minutes

Serves: 4

2 eggplants

45ml / 1½fl. oz olive oil

3 medium tomatoes, seeded and diced

1 cup mozzarella cheese, finely diced

2 tbsp basil leaves, chopped

salt and freshly ground black pepper

extra basil leaves, for serving

Dressing:

4 tbsp olive oil

1 tomato, diced

1 tbsp balsamic vinegar

2 tbsp pine nuts, toasted

salt and black pepper

Remove the stalks from the eggplants and slice them lengthwise in thin sections. Brush the slices on both sides with oil and grill both sides until soft and beginning to brown.

Preheat the oven to 180°C (350F). In a bowl, combine the tomatoes, mozzarella, basil and seasoning. Spoon a little onto the end of each slice of eggplant and roll up. Place it seam-side down in a greased, ovenproof dish and bake for 15–17 minutes.

In a small pan, using a little of the oil, sauté the tomato until softened. Add the remaining oil, vinegar and pine nuts, and gently warm through. Season to taste. Arrange the eggplant rolls on a platter and spoon the dressing over them.

Honey Gammon with Pineapple Salsa

Prepared cook time: 25 minutes   Serves: 4

4 thick smoked ham steaks,
225g/9oz each

2 sprigs fresh thyme

1 tbsp clear honey

lime wedge, to serve

coriander (cilantro), leaves to
garnish

Salsa:

2 tomatoes

225g/9oz pineapple, cut into
1cm/⅓in cubes

1 clove of garlic, crushed

1 red chilli, deseeded and
chopped

2 tbsp extra virgin olive oil

juiced ½ lime

2 tbsp chopped coriander
(cilantro) leaves

salt and black pepper

First make the salsa. Put the tomatoes in a bowl and cover with boiling water. Leave for 30 seconds, then skin, deseed and dice. Combine the tomatoes with the pineapple, garlic, chilli, oil, lime juice and coriander (cilantro). Season to taste and set aside.

Preheat the grill to high. Score the fat around the edge of each steak and rub all over with the thyme sprigs. Brush the gammon with honey for 2–3 minutes each side, until tender and cooked through. Serve with the salsa and lime wedges and garnish with the coriander (cilantro).

Chicken with Tarragon Cream Sauce

Prep and cook time: 45 minutes

Serves: 4

4 large skinless, boneless chicken breasts

8 sundried tomatoes in oil, drained

8 slices rindless smoked bacon

2 tbsps olive oil

455g/1lb baby leeks

1½ cups fresh chicken stock

2 tbsps brandy

⅔ cup light cream

2 tbsps chopped fresh tarragon, plus extra to garnish

salt and black pepper

Preheat the oven to 200°C (400F). Cut a deep slice into 1 side of each chicken breast to make a pocket. Place 2 tomatoes in each pocket, then wrap 2 bacon slices around each breast. Secure with cocktail stalks.

Heat 1 tablespoon of the oil in an ovenproof frying pan. Cook the chicken for 2–3 minutes, turning once, until browned all over. Transfer to the oven and cook for 15 minutes, or until the chicken is cooked through. Transfer to a plate, remove the cocktail stalks and keep warm. Meanwhile, preheat the grill to high. Brush the leeks with the remaining oil and grill for 6–8 minutes, until softened.

Add the stock and brandy to the pan. Cook over a high heat for 3 minutes, stirring and scraping, until reduced by half. Beat in the cream and tarragon and simmer for 2–3 minutes, until slightly thickened. Season, then spoon over the chicken parcels and leeks. Garnish with the reserved tarragon.

Deep-Fried Okra

Prep and cook time: 7 minutes   Serves: 4

225g / 9oz okra
1 egg
1 cup flour
1 cup ice-cold water
oil, for frying

Garlic Walnut Sauce:
2 slices bread
½ cup water
½ cup walnuts
2 cloves of garlic, chopped
2 tbsp white-wine vinegar
1 tbsp olive oil
salt and black pepper to taste

To make the garlic walnut sauce, soak the bread in water for 5 minutes. Squeeze out the water. Place the walnuts in a blender, and process until finely chopped. Add the bread, garlic and vinegar. Process until combined. While the motor is running, add the olive oil, salt and pepper and process until a paste is formed.

Wash and trim the okra. In a large bowl, beat the egg until frothy, add the flour and water and beat together until the batter is also frothy.

Heat the oil in a large pan, dip the okra in the batter and cook in the oil for 1–2 minutes, or until lightly brown.

Drain on absorbent paper and serve with the lemon wedges and the garlic walnut sauce.

Raspberry and Elderflower Fool

Prep and cook time: 45 minutes   Serves: 6

3 cups raspberries, defrosted if frozen, plus extra to decorate

60ml / 2fl. oz elderflower cordial

60g / 2oz icing (confectioners') sugar, plus extra to dust

2 cups cream

fresh mint to decorate

Purée the raspberries and cordial until smooth in a blender. Blend in the icing sugar. Spoon 1 tablespoon of the mixture into each dessert glass, reserving the remaining purée, and set aside.

Beat the cream until it is stiff, then gradually fold into the reserved raspberry purée.

Spoon the raspberry cream into the glasses and chill in the fridge for 30 minutes. Serve decorated with the extra raspberries and mint and dusted with the icing sugar.

Grilled Peaches with Sweet Brioche

Prep and cook time: 25 minutes   Serves: 4

4 large, ripe peaches, halved and stoned
1 tbsp clear honey
90g / 3oz unsalted butter
2 medium eggs, lightly beaten
2 tbsp sweet white wine
2 tbsp caster (superfine) sugar
1 tbsp lemon juice
a pinch of ground cinnamon
4 slices brioche
crème fraîche to serve

Preheat the grill to medium. Place the peach halves, cut-side up, on the grill and top each with a drizzle of honey and a knob of butter, reserving half the butter for frying. Grill for 5–6 minutes, until softened and golden.

Beat together the eggs, wine, sugar, lemon juice and cinnamon. Dip the slices of brioche in the egg mixture to coat.

Melt the remaining butter in a large pan and gently fry the brioche slices for 2–3 minutes each side, until crisp and golden. Top each slice with 2 peach halves and their juice and a spoonful of crème fraîche.